NATURE'S WRATH
THE SCIENCE BEHIND NATURAL DISASTERS

THE SCIENCE OF
EARTHQUAKES

MATT ANNISS

Gareth Stevens
Publishing

Please visit our website, www.garethstevens.com. For a free color catalog of all our high-quality books, call toll free 1-800-542-2595 or fax 1-877-542-2596.

Library of Congress Cataloging-in-Publication Data

Anniss, Matt.
The science of earthquakes / Matt Anniss.
    p. cm. — (Nature's wrath)
 Includes index.
ISBN 978-1-4339-8656-7 (pbk.)
ISBN 978-1-4339-8657-4 (6-pack)
ISBN 978-1-4339-8655-0 (library binding)
1. Earthquakes. I. Title. II. Series: Nature's wrath.
 QE543.3.A56 2013
 511.22—dc23

2012025889

First Edition

Published in 2013 by
Gareth Stevens Publishing
111 East 14th Street, Suite 349
New York, NY 10003

Produced by Calcium, www.calciumcreative.co.uk
Designed by Simon Borrough and Nick Leggett
Edited by Sarah Eason and Vicky Egan
Picture research by Susannah Jayes

Photo credits: Cover: Top: Shutterstock: iBird; Bottom (l to r): Shutterstock: fpolat69; Dreamstime: David Snyder; Wikipedia: Lkluft 8; FEMA News Photo; Shutterstock: Wanghanan. Inside: Dreamstime: Arindam Banerjee 19, Marcelo Vildósola Garrigó 29, Walter Graneri 33, Sadık Güleç 16, 18, 34, Mingchai Law 26, Irfan Nurdiansyah 35, Semnic 7, Chatchai Somwat 24, Nigel Spiers 1b, 36-37, 37, 38l, Anthony Aneese Totah Jr 30l, Yekaixp 17, 27c, Concetta Zingale 21br; FEMA News Photo: 12cl, 12-13, Robert A. Eplett 11b; Shutterstock: Alexandralaw1977 38tr, Arindam Banerjee 4, ChameleonsEye 1t, 40, Robert Crow 30-31, Fpolat69 5, Chris Geszvain 9, M. Bonotto 40-41, Petrafier 45, Tom Pingel 28, SeanPavonePhoto 31cr, SSguy 42, St.Nick 42-43, Przemek Tokar 15tr, Visdia 6, Worldpics 44; USAID: 20cl, 23tr; US Navy: Mass Communications Specialist 2nd Class Eric C.Tretter 21cl, 22, 23cl; Wikipedia: ChiefHira 25, Gabriel 39tr, Gedstrom 10tr, Lkluft 8, Nowozin 14-15, TheWiz83 32.

Printed in the United States of America

CPSIA compliance information: Batch #CW13GS: For further information contact Gareth Stevens, New York, New York at 1-800-542-2595.

CONTENTS

WHAT IS AN EARTHQUAKE?

An earthquake occurs when pressure inside Earth builds up to such an extent that it can no longer be contained. Earthquakes happen every day around the world. Many are small and barely noticeable. Others make the ground move so violently that buildings shake, trees fall to the ground, and rivers burst their banks.

The effects of an earthquake can be devastating. When a powerful earthquake struck Haiti in 2010, many children were left orphaned.

Dangerous Force

Some earthquakes last for just a few seconds and may do no more damage than to displace a few roof tiles. Others last for longer than a minute, shaking the ground violently and making buildings crumble. Each year there are 100,000 severe earthquakes. Together they cause billions of dollars worth of damage to buildings, highways, and bridges.

Earthquakes can destroy buildings and cars within a few seconds. The cost of repairing the damage can run to billions of dollars.

Millions at Risk

Many people die each year as a direct result of earthquakes and the damage they cause to towns and villages. Billions of people in earthquake-prone places around the world live with the risk that an earthquake can suddenly strike and cause devastation in a matter of a few seconds.

Constant Threat

Earthquakes are one of the most common of natural disasters. They occur on every continent, although some places in the world are more likely to experience a big earthquake than others. Although we can prepare for earthquakes, we cannot stop them. They can strike, without warning, at any time.

WORLD'S WORST

The most devastating earthquake of the last 100 years took place in the Tangshan province of China. At 3:42 a.m. on July 28, 1976, a massive earthquake shook the ground for 23 seconds. Just 16 hours later, an "aftershock" quake also rocked the province. More than 240,000 people died in the disaster.

CHAPTER ONE

THE SCIENCE OF EARTHQUAKES

The surface of our planet is made up of a number of huge pieces of rock that fit together a little like the pieces of a jigsaw puzzle. These pieces are called tectonic plates. The plates are many thousands of miles long and wide, and nearly 20,000 feet (6,000 m) deep. They move very, very slowly—usually only 1 to 2 inches (3 to 6 cm) a year. The point at which tectonic plates meet is called a fault, or fault line.

The fiery lines on this image show some of Earth's fault lines.

MOVING EARTH

Occasionally, two tectonic plates will rub together along a fault line. The resistance between the two surfaces creates friction, and this sends waves of energy, known as seismic waves, upward toward the surface of the earth. When these waves of energy reach the surface, they cause the ground to shake and tremble—and this is what we call an earthquake. The point at which the waves reach the surface is known as the "epicenter." This is where the earthquake is at its most powerful. The epicenter is vertically above the earthquake's "focus" (also known as the "hypocenter"). Shock waves move outward from the epicenter and cause the ground to shake for hundreds or even thousands of miles around.

WORLD'S WORST

The most devastating earthquake took place in Shaanxi in central China, in 1556. The huge quake caused the deaths of more than 800,000 people. At the time, many people in the region were living in man-made caves that collapsed when the earthquake hit, killing those inside.

When two fault lines rub together, huge cracks in the ground many miles deep can suddenly appear.

TECTONIC PLATES

The role of tectonic plates and fault lines in causing earthquakes cannot be underestimated. The movements of Earth's shifting plates can cause dramatic changes to the surface structure of the planet. While not all earthquakes happen close to fault lines, the most damaging events happen at these natural boundaries.

Seen from above, the bumpy ridge of the San Andreas Fault line rises up from Earth's surface like a backbone.

Earth's Jigsaw Puzzle

The surface of the earth is made up of 15 tectonic plates of different sizes. They fit together like a jigsaw—each piece slots into another to make up the surface of the planet. The points at which the plates touch see the most "seismic activity," the rubbing that creates earthquakes on Earth's surface.

Where Fault Lines Meet

All over our planet, there are fault lines where tectonic plates touch. Some are at the bottom of major oceans, such as the Atlantic or Pacific, while others can be seen on the surface of the earth. A famous example is the legendary San Andreas Fault, which runs from the tip of South America all the way to Canada via the West Coast of the United States.

The devastating power of tectonic plate movement was shown in Asia on March 11, 2011, when Japan suffered one of the worst earthquakes in its history. The quake was one of the most destructive ever recorded and nearly 30,000 buildings collapsed. Around 15,000 people died, with 26,000 more injured.

Danger Zones

Areas of the earth where many fault lines come together are most at risk of experiencing devastating earthquakes. Scientists call the area around Japan and the Far East the Pacific "Ring of Fire," because it sits at the joining point of five different tectonic plates. Within this 25,000-mile (40,000 km) zone, 90 percent of the world's earthquakes take place.

The dramatic landscape that surrounds the San Andreas Fault zone was created over millions of years by the movement of tectonic plates.

REAL-LIFE SCIENCE
LOS ANGELES, 1994

When the residents of Northridge, a suburb of Los Angeles, California, went to bed on the evening of Sunday, January 16, 1994, there was nothing to suggest that many would soon be fighting for their lives. It was a peaceful evening and the suburb was relatively quiet. All that was soon to change. At 4:31 a.m. on January 17, a violent earthquake struck the neighborhood without warning.

Terror in the Night

For between 10 and 20 seconds, the ground shook violently. Woken from deep sleep, people's reactions were slower than they might have been in the day. As if in a nightmare, they found their homes destroyed. Many did not have a chance to take cover, let alone escape from the mountains of rubble that came crashing down all around them. Sixteen people died almost instantly when their apartment block collapsed, and hundreds of others were injured, many badly.

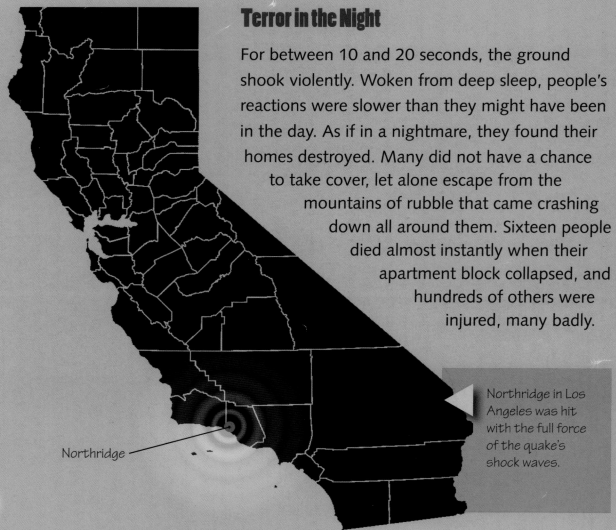

Northridge

Northridge in Los Angeles was hit with the full force of the quake's shock waves.

Many street surfaces were ripped apart by the powerful earthquake that struck Los Angeles in 1994.

Damage to the Community

The earthquake hit Northridge hard. Although Reseda, another neighborhood in the San Fernando Valley, was later pinpointed as the epicenter of the quake, Northridge was the area that was most badly damaged by the sudden event.

Al McNeil watched as his home was destroyed by a fire caused by the violent Los Angeles earthquake:

"The whole street was on fire. Even the tall palm trees were burning. It was a very frightening experience. We lost everything. We have nothing, but nobody was hurt."

The exterior walls of apartments and homes collapsed in the earthquake, leaving buildings devastated.

HITTING NORTHRIDGE

Northridge is around 20 miles (31 km) from downtown Los Angeles, which also sustained damage. In fact, buildings and roads were damaged up to 85 miles (125 km) from the epicenter. Parts of the Santa Monica Freeway, known as the busiest highway in the United States, collapsed or were badly damaged, and 11 hospitals had to be evacuated for fear of collapse.

After the earthquake destroyed their homes, many people had to rescue what they could from the wreckage.

The Day of the Earthquake

JAN 17, 1994 4:31 a.m.
A massive earthquake lasting between 10 and 20 seconds strikes Reseda, a neighborhood of Los Angeles, in the San Fernando Valley. A second quake (or aftershock) follows.

Within seconds, the overpass bridges of Interstate 10 on the Santa Monica Freeway—the busiest freeway in the United States—are reduced to rubble. Northridge Meadows apartment complex collapses, killing 16 people.

4:35 a.m.
Emergency services receive the first calls from the injured and get reports of damaged buildings.

4:45 a.m.
Emergency services head out to the affected areas.

5:45 a.m.
Los Angeles' Mayor Richard J. Riordan declares a state of emergency for the city, and an evening curfew is imposed. He works closely with Police Chief Willie Williams to coordinate the rescue efforts.

The force of the earthquake was so strong that sections of the Santa Monica Freeway collapsed.

Widespread Tremors

The earthquake was so violent that it could be felt over 200 miles (320 km) away in Las Vegas, Nevada. In total, thousands of buildings over a wide area were damaged or destroyed by the quake. The official death toll was 57, and over 8,700 people were injured. It is estimated that the cost of repairing the damage came to over $20 billion, making it the costliest earthquake in US history.

Australian tourist Nick Stevens was very lucky to escape the earthquake:

"The earthquake was a 6.5 on the Richter scale but a 10 on my fear scale. We had been planning to go to Universal Studios, where they have the earthquake ride. Now we won't have to bother."

Survivors Speak

6:45 a.m.
Reports come in of 50 buildings on fire. Water and gas pipes have burst. Electricity is down in some areas. The airport is closed due to lack of power. With hospitals damaged, doctors operate outdoors.

9:05 a.m.
California Governor Pete Wilson declares a state of emergency.

9:45 a.m.
Emergency services finally get all fires in the neighborhood under control.

2:08 p.m.
President Bill Clinton declares a "natural disaster" for Los Angeles County.

7:00 p.m.
Work begins clearing debris from streets, and demolition of highways begins.

JAN 18, 1994
Many badly damaged streets around the city are closed for safety reasons. Cleanup operations throughout the city and beyond begin in earnest.

EARTHQUAKE TRIGGERS

Most earthquakes occur naturally, but some are triggered by things that people do. Deep mining, building dams, and geothermal electricity power plants have all been linked to "induced seismicity," the process of accidentally creating earthquakes.

Under Pressure

Earthquakes happen when pressure is applied to Earth's crust by tectonic plates rubbing together. However, human-induced pressure on the rock deep beneath us can have the same effect, triggering an earthquake.

Dam Danger

New dams can trigger earthquakes. Once a new dam or reservoir has been built, it is filled with water. The weight of the water places a lot of pressure on the ground and rocks below. If this pressure becomes too great, it is released in the form of seismic waves at a nearby fault line, and an earthquake can occur. Scientists say that if we keep building bigger dams, one of them may one day trigger a catastrophic earthquake.

WORLD'S WORST

In 1967, 180 people died and 1,500 were injured following a very violent earthquake in Maharashtra, India. Afterward, scientists discovered that the epicenter of the earthquake was directly below the Koyna Dam reservoir.

Geothermal Link to Earthquakes

Another activity linked to induced seismicity is the use of geothermal energy to generate electricity. Geothermal energy is heat from Earth's core that finds its way to the surface in the form of steam. The techniques used to harness geothermal energy have been linked to an increase in minor earthquakes. The problem is most noticeable in the area surrounding The Geysers in California, the world's largest complex of geothermal electricity power plants.

Digging for coal in mines with large drilling machines is one of the man-made activities linked to induced seismic activity.

The giant Three Gorges Dam in China is one of the largest dams in the world. Scientists believe that enormous dams such as this could be linked to seismic activity that results in earthquakes.

CHAPTER TWO

THE COST OF EARTHQUAKES

Earthquakes are among the most devastating natural events on Earth. Extremely violent earthquakes occur relatively infrequently. However, even modest quakes can cause huge damage, especially if the shock waves strike areas where many people live.

A major earthquake hit Turkey in 2011, destroying homes and forcing people to live in tent cities, such as the one above, for weeks.

DEATH AND DESTRUCTION

When the ground shakes violently during an earthquake, it can cause massive damage to buildings. The force of the earth's movement weakens the buildings' foundations and causes them to collapse. In wealthy countries, such as the United States and Japan, buildings are often designed to withstand earthquakes. In poor countries, which have little money to spend on earthquake-proof buildings, the potential for massive loss of life and homes is huge. Severe earthquakes also cause disruption to electricity, water, and gas supplies. This can cause huge fires to break out, which in turn cause even more death and destruction.

WORLD'S WORST

Many people in Turkey suffered the effects of poorly built housing when an earthquake hit the city of Izmit on August 17, 1999. Over 17,000 people died in the earthquake. More than 120,000 homes were destroyed, leaving half a million people homeless.

Without fresh water, people are forced to drink whatever water they can find. When this happens, it's not long before sickness and dangerous diseases spread quickly through already shattered communities.

Buildings that have not been built to withstand earthquakes are often reduced to rubble when a severe earthquake strikes. Entire towns can be destroyed, leaving many people homeless.

DEATH AND DISEASE

If earthquakes cause chaos even in wealthy countries such as the United States, the devastation in poor countries can be of incredible proportions. Added to that, the problems that occur after the earthquake can be as significant as the disaster itself. With police, firefighters, doctors, and nurses in short supply, there is little to stop dangerous diseases spreading and killing thousands.

Receiving aid, such as clean drinking water, quickly can make the difference between life and death for the victims of earthquakes.

Water for Life

We all need water to live. When earthquake damage cuts off fresh water supplies, and aid is unavailable, people are forced to drink whatever water they can find. They often drink from untreated water supplies, such as rivers and lakes, which can make people sick.

Dirty Water

When water is not clean, it can contain germs that cause disease. The water is effectively poisoned. Dangerous diseases such as cholera, dysentery, and the *E.coli* virus are often found in dirty water. An outbreak of any one of these diseases can make thousands of people incredibly sick. In poor areas where treatment, doctors, and nurses are scarce, people often die.

In poor countries struck by earthquakes, dirty water supplies such as this one may be the only option for survivors.

Dead Bodies

Being close to dead bodies is another way to catch diseases. After an earthquake in a poor country, bodies may be piled up in the streets or in open graves by the side of the road. For people living there, it is impossible to avoid contamination, and epidemics of disease often follow the disaster of the earthquake itself.

REAL-LIFE SCIENCE
HAITI, 2010

Haiti is one of the poorest nations on Earth. Underdeveloped and frequently torn apart by civil war, it has seen many disasters over the years. One of the worst disasters to hit the island was a huge earthquake on Tuesday, January 12, 2010.

National Disaster

At just before 5:00 p.m., the ground started violently shaking in the capital, Port-au-Prince. The earthquake's epicenter was just 15.5 miles (25 km) away, so the city felt the full force of its power. Most of the buildings in the city were poorly built and unable to withstand the shaking. By the time the ground stopped moving, Port-au-Prince had been reduced to rubble.

Port-au-Prince was severely hit by the earthquake, which destroyed much of the capital.

Rescue workers pulled some lucky survivors from the wreckage of the Haiti earthquake.

Port-au-Prince

Total Destruction

More than 188,000 houses were damaged and 105,000 were destroyed by the Haiti earthquake, leaving 1.5 million people homeless. The quake left 62 million cubic feet (19 million cu m) of rubble and debris in Port-au-Prince—enough to fill a line of shipping containers stretching from the United Kingdom to the Middle East.

Sandra Félicien lost her husband in the Haiti disaster. Describing the desperate conditions she and her 6-year-old son were forced to live in after the quake she said:

"We are so powerless. It is like bobbing along on the waves of the ocean, waiting to be saved."

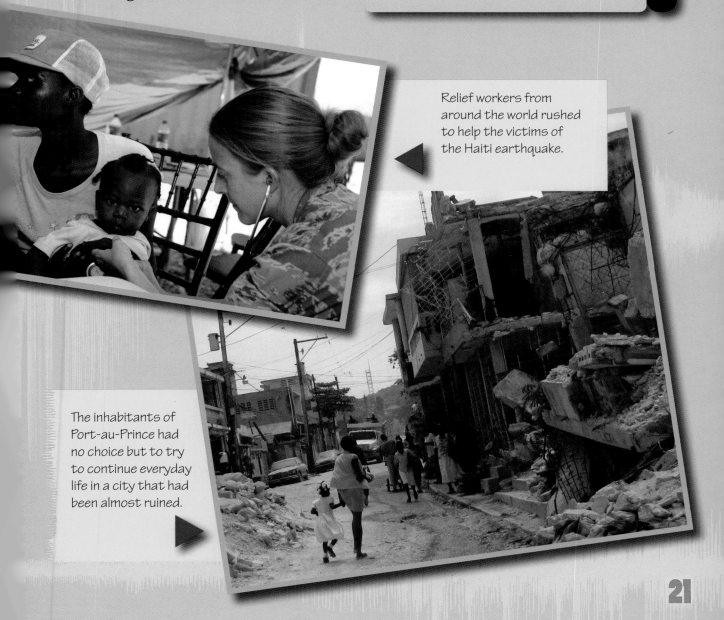

Relief workers from around the world rushed to help the victims of the Haiti earthquake.

The inhabitants of Port-au-Prince had no choice but to try to continue everyday life in a city that had been almost ruined.

HELPING HAITI

The Haitian government appealed to the world for help immediately. The country's emergency services were simply not equipped to cope with such a major disaster. The United States sent troops to help with the relief effort, and many other nations provided specialist search and rescue teams.

The World Reacts

President Obama described the situation in Haiti as "truly heart wrenching," and, along with other nations, promised aid. Within hours, rescue teams from around the world were flying to the disaster.

> People were without food and fresh drinking water for days following the disaster. Army helicopters airlifted supplies to Haiti's worst-hit areas.

Events as They Happened

JAN 12, 2010
A massive earthquake strikes 15.5 miles (25 km) outside of Port-au-Prince. Tremors are felt as far away as Cuba and Jamaica.

JAN 13, 2010
Haiti's government appeals for help with the search and rescue operation, fresh water, and medical supplies.

JAN 14, 2010
President Obama pledges more than $100 million and the help of thousands of US troops.

JAN 15, 2010
Rescue workers find a 2-year-old girl alive in a ruined school. The UN launches an appeal to raise $550 million for relief aid.

JAN 16, 2010
Refugee camps are set up outside Port-au-Prince. With local cemeteries full, the government resorts to burying bodies in mass graves. The US Federal Aviation Administration helps to improve the flow of air traffic moving in and out of the airport.

JAN 17, 2010
With the parliament building and presidential palace both destroyed, the Haitian government finds a temporary base at a run-down police station on the outskirts of the city of Port-au-Prince.

Death Toll

It quickly became clear that the devastating earthquake in Haiti was one of the most destructive on record. When the dust had settled, more than 316,000 people had died, many crushed by collapsed buildings. To add to the disaster, the millions of people made homeless were then ravaged by diseases, such as cholera.

Search and rescue teams worked through the night to try to find survivors.

US Navy personnel were deployed to deliver water, food, and medicine to earthquake-stricken Haiti.

21-year-old Geffard Guliene was forced to flee Port-au-Prince after losing her home in the devastating earthquake:

"I can't stay here anymore. We are living like animals here. The smell is awful and infection is setting in. The kids are in trauma."

Survivors Speak

JAN 18, 2010
Chaos erupts at Port-au-Prince airport as international planes full of food and medical supplies begin to land. The United Nations says that it could take "decades" to rebuild Haiti following the huge earthquake.

JAN 19, 2010
The United Nations sends more soldiers to Port-au-Prince after violence erupts on the city's streets.

JAN 20, 2010
A second strong earthquake hits Haiti, causing more damage. Survivors are evacuated from Port-au-Prince.

JAN 27, 2010
Rescue workers pull a 16-year-old girl from rubble 15 days after she was buried alive.

FEB 1, 2010
Rock and pop stars Akon, Lionel Ritchie, and Celine Dion join forces to record a song to raise money for the earthquake relief effort.

FEB 10, 2010
Incredibly, a 28-year-old man is pulled out weak but still alive from the remains of a building, 27 days after the first earthquake struck.

FURTHER DAMAGE

Many earthquakes are so powerful that they can weaken the ground beneath us. Two things may happen as a result—soil may turn to mud (soil liquefaction) and landslides can occur, with part of a cliff or mountain sliding downhill.

Liquid Ground

If the ground contains a lot of water, for example in sandy or muddy places, the soil can turn to liquid. When this happens, the ground becomes weak and unstable. Any buildings may sink into the liquefied ground and, lacking a strong foundation, collapse.

One of the worst cases of soil liquefaction followed the 1964 Good Friday earthquake in Alaska. As buildings sunk into the ground, collapsed, or were covered by landslides, 143 people died across the state. Tsunamis then also destroyed buildings on the coast.

Devastating floods often follow powerful quakes. Survivors of the earthquake may then instead become the victims of an overwhelming flow of water.

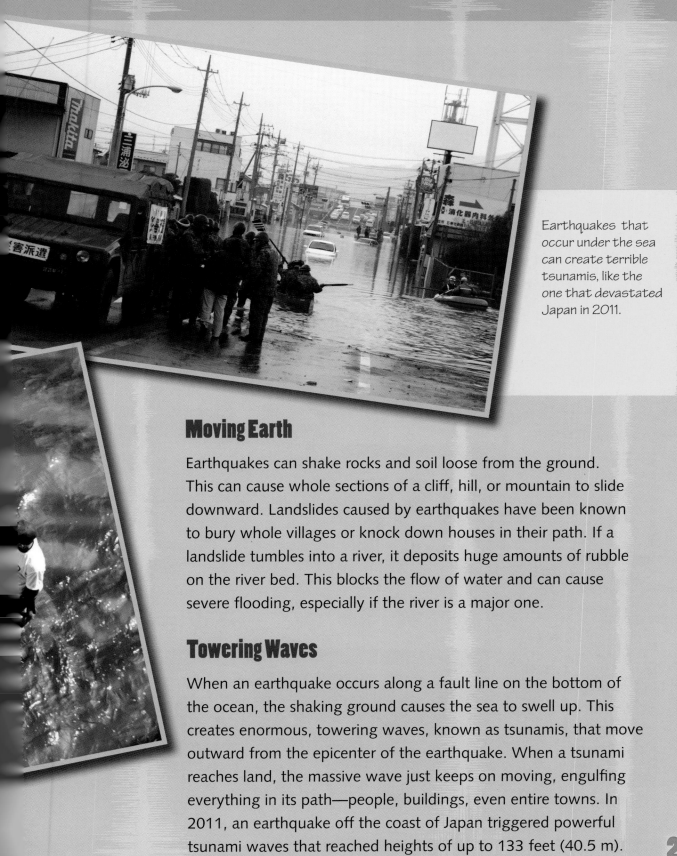

Earthquakes that occur under the sea can create terrible tsunamis, like the one that devastated Japan in 2011.

Moving Earth

Earthquakes can shake rocks and soil loose from the ground. This can cause whole sections of a cliff, hill, or mountain to slide downward. Landslides caused by earthquakes have been known to bury whole villages or knock down houses in their path. If a landslide tumbles into a river, it deposits huge amounts of rubble on the river bed. This blocks the flow of water and can cause severe flooding, especially if the river is a major one.

Towering Waves

When an earthquake occurs along a fault line on the bottom of the ocean, the shaking ground causes the sea to swell up. This creates enormous, towering waves, known as tsunamis, that move outward from the epicenter of the earthquake. When a tsunami reaches land, the massive wave just keeps on moving, engulfing everything in its path—people, buildings, even entire towns. In 2011, an earthquake off the coast of Japan triggered powerful tsunami waves that reached heights of up to 133 feet (40.5 m).

AFTERSHOCKS

When a major earthquake strikes, it can cause many catastrophic events. By far the worst are aftershocks. Just like earthquakes, aftershocks are unpredictable. They can happen anywhere along the same fault line that caused the earthquake. Aftershocks are the movements of the tectonic plates that caused the earthquake as they settle into their new, post-quake positions.

After the devastating 2011 Japan earthquake, many people took shelter in subway stations to keep safe from the aftershocks that followed.

ISP 池袋ショッピングパーク
Ikebukuro Shopping Park

BANK セブン銀行ATM   みずほ銀行   CRE SAI

Minor to Severe Aftershocks

How severe the first aftershock is usually depends on how powerful the original earthquake was. If it was a particularly violent earthquake, the first aftershock is likely to be only a little less powerful than the original quake. In the case of devastating earthquakes, there may be a number of big aftershocks in the 2 hours following the quake.

Thousands of people slept outdoors after the 2011 earthquake in Japan. It was safer to be outside than to risk sheltering in buildings constantly shaken by the aftershocks that followed the enormous earthquake.

Shocks Years Later

Sometimes, aftershocks can be felt for years after a major earthquake. Scientists believe that minor earthquakes regularly felt around the New Madrid fault line between St. Louis and Memphis in the southern and midwestern United States are actually aftershocks from a devastating earthquake that hit the region over 200 years ago. Over time, aftershocks reduce in power, eventually becoming little more than minor events that may hardly be felt.

CHAPTER THREE

STUDYING EARTHQUAKES

The study of earthquakes is called "seismology." Scientists who study earthquakes are called "seismologists." They use a range of computer equipment and software to detect and monitor seismic waves. There are two main types of seismic waves. Body waves move underground, and surface waves move across Earth's surface.

Seismograph machines detect ground tremors that are linked to imminent earthquakes.

SEISMOLOGY

Seismic waves are detected using a machine called a seismograph (or seismometer). The machine is connected to an instrument buried very deep under the ground that measures seismic waves. Any movement produces a wave-like graph on a computer screen. Seismographs enable seismologists to accurately rate the strength (magnitude) of an earthquake using the Richter scale. This rates earthquakes on a sliding scale from 1 to 10. A magnitude 5 earthquake would cause light damage to a house, while one rated 7 or 8 could cause widespread devastation. There are, on average, 15 magnitude 7 earthquakes each year. Magnitude 10 has never been recorded.

WORLD'S WORST

The worst quake ever recorded happened near Lumaco, Chile, on May 22, 1960. It was recorded at 9.5 on the Richter scale. Around 3,000 people died as a result of the earthquake, which sent a 33-foot (10 m) high tsunami sweeping across the Pacific Ocean.

Chile is one of the most earthquake-prone countries on Earth. In 2007, another earthquake hit the country, destroying towns such as this one below.

FORECASTING DISASTER

Earthquakes by their very nature are unpredictable. Because of this, accurately predicting when they may strike a particular region is incredibly difficult. However, scientists have developed methods of detection that make some early warnings possible.

Early Warning

Japan and Mexico are two countries frequently devastated by major earthquakes. Scientists there have developed advanced early warning systems to alert people to potential forthcoming events. They carefully monitor seismic wave activity and study images beamed down by satellites to detect movement in the earth's tectonic plates. They also look out for other signs of earthquakes, such as changes in the tides along their coastlines.

QUE HACER EN: / WHAT TO DO IN:
SISMO - EARTHQUAKE

1 CONSERVE LA CALMA / STAY CALM

2 ELIMINE FUENTES DE INCENDIO / GET AWAY FROM THINGS THAT CAN ORIGINATE FIRE

3 RETIRESE DE VENTANAS Y OBJETOS QUE PUEDAN CAER / GET AWAY FROM WINDOWS AND OBJECTS THAT COULD FALL

4 NO USE ELEVADORES / DO NOT USE ELEVATORS

5 UBIQUESE EN ZONAS DE SEGURIDAD / STAY IN SECURITY ZONES

6 LOCALICE LA RUTA DE EVACUACION / FOLLOW SIGNS TO FOUND EMERGENCY EXITS

QUE HACER EN: / WHAT TO DO IN:
INCENDIO - FIRE

1 CONSERVE LA CALMA / STAY CALM

2 IDENTIFIQUE QUE ORIGINA EL INCENDIO / IDENTIFY WHAT IS ORIGINATING THE FIRE

3 EMITA LA ALARMA / TURN ON THE FIRE ALARM

4 USE EL EXTINTOR / USE THE FIRE EXTINGUISHER

5 OBEDEZCA INDICACIONES DEL PERSONAL CAPACITADO / FOLLOW OUR PERSONNEL INSTRUCTIONS

6 SI PUEDE AYUDE SI NO RETIRESE / HELP OR LEAVE THE BUILDING

7 NO USE ELEVADORES / DO NOT USE ELEVATORS

8 HUMEDEZCA UN TRAPO Y CUBRA NARIZ Y BOCA / TAKE A WET TOWEL AND COVER YOUR MOUTH AND NOSE

9 SI EL HUMO ES DENSO ARRASTRESE POR EL SUELO / IF THE FIRE SMOKE IS HEAVY LAY DOWN ON THE FLOOR AND LOOK FOR AN EXIT

In Mexico, where earthquakes are common, buildings contain instructions that tell people what to do in the event of an earthquake strike.

On Alert

If significant seismic activity is detected close to a fault line, scientists quickly alert the government. They then put out an earthquake alert using the local television and radio channels. In Japan, earthquake alerts are sent to all cell phones via text messages. Some cities, such as Tokyo, also have outdoor warning sirens.

Learning from the Past

Another method used to predict earthquakes involves looking at the history books. By looking at how often earthquakes have occurred over a long period of time, scientists can work out the likelihood of another devastating event happening. Scientists in California have worked out that the probability of a catastrophic earthquake hitting San Francisco in the next 30 years is 63 percent.

Kobe, in Japan, is ready for any potential earthquake. The local Earthquake Warning System alerts people in the city to any imminent danger.

San Francisco lies on the San Andreas Fault line. Its position on the volatile fault line makes it particularly vulnerable to earthquakes.

WORLD'S WORST

In 1988, scientists said that a major earthquake would hit Lorma Prieta near San Francisco in early 1989. Although their prediction was inaccurate, an earthquake measuring 6.9 on the Richter scale did hit San Francisco in October 1989, killing 63 people.

WRONG CALLS

The science of earthquake prediction is a relatively new one. To date, very few people have accurately predicted where and when an earthquake will strike, although many have tried. The history books are full of strange and unlikely calls, only a few of which were correct.

Many great historic buildings were destroyed when an earthquake hit L'Aquila in central Italy in 2009.

Right Call, Wrong Place

Italian police charged a scientist named Giampaolo Giuliani for spreading fear when he predicted that a major earthquake would devastate the town of Sulmona in northern Italy, in March 2009. Although he was wrong, a catastrophic earthquake did hit nearby L'Aquila, just 30 miles (50 km) from Sulmona, on April 6, 2009.

No-show Earthquake

In June 1981, a scientist at the US Bureau of Mines predicted that an earthquake would strike the city of Lima, Peru. Hundreds of thousands of people fled the city in a panic, but the earthquake never materialized.

The L'Aquila earthquake was one of the most powerful ever recorded in Italy. Measuring 5.8 on the Richter scale, it destroyed much of the ancient city. Centuries-old buildings collapsed, killing 308 people. It was the first earthquake to hit the city for more than 300 years.

Rescue workers searched the wrecked buildings of L'Aquila following the devastating earthquake that struck the town. In 2011, another severe earthquake hit northern Italy, near Bologna.

Animal Warnings

Some people have observed that before an earthquake, animals begin to behave oddly. In 1974, the Chinese National Earthquake Bureau believed that a major earthquake was on the way, so it asked people to notify them of any strange animal behavior. In December, they started to receive reports of pigs digging burrows and geese flying into trees. They decided to evacuate the city of Haicheng on February 3, 1975. It was the right decision. The next morning, a devastating 7.3 magnitude earthquake destroyed 50 percent of the city. The evacuation saved 150,000 lives.

CHAPTER FOUR

FIGHTING NATURE

Governments in countries close to fault lines go to great lengths to try to minimize the potential damage from earthquakes. As well as using early warning systems and paying for scientists to monitor seismic activity, they also make sure buildings are "earthquake proof" and teach people how best to act in the event of an earthquake.

Rescue workers are trained to use specialized machinery to cut through the wreckage created by earthquakes in order to reach the victims beneath.

BE PREPARED

In earthquake zones, homes, offices, and other structures are specially built to withstand the ferocious shaking of a major earthquake. If buildings can withstand the shaking, it dramatically cuts down the loss of life caused by an earthquake. Many governments now also teach their citizens what to do in the event of an earthquake. If people know what action to take the moment an earthquake strikes, it can save their lives. Governments also prepare for earthquakes by having an Emergency Management Plan. Police, hospitals, and fire services plan in advance how they would respond. More lives will be saved if their response is quick and efficient.

WORLD'S WORST

In December 1988, an earthquake registering 7.1 on the Richter scale hit the city of Spitak, Armenia. Due to poor quality buildings, almost the entire city was reduced to rubble. At least 25,000 people died, making it one of the most destructive events in Armenian history.

Skyscrapers dominate the skylines of modern Japanese cities. Modern buildings in Japan, such as the ACT Tower in the city of Hamamatsu, have been designed to withstand the force of earthquakes.

35

REAL-LIFE SCIENCE
NEW ZEALAND, 2011

On September 4, 2010, a powerful earthquake struck the Canterbury region of New Zealand's South Island. The city of Christchurch, situated just 12 miles (20 km) from the earthquake's epicenter, sustained some damage, but no one was killed. New Zealanders breathed a sigh of relief. Then, 6 months later, another earthquake struck the city. This time, they weren't so lucky.

The earthquake struck at a depth of 3 miles (5 km) below the surface of the ground and 12 miles (20 km) southeast of Christchurch.

Christchurch, South Island

Second Earthquake

It was lunchtime on February 22, 2011, when the next earthquake struck. With a magnitude of 6.3 on the Richter scale, it was powerful enough to cause widespread damage to buildings and roads. A large number of Christchurch's buildings, already weakened by the earthquake 6 months earlier, collapsed or fell in on themselves. Two buses, packed with lunchtime passengers, were crushed by falling rubble. The 6-story Canterbury Television Building was reduced to little more than a pile of bricks and dust. Ninety people were trapped inside when it collapsed. None survived.

Dealing with the Disaster

As fires broke out in the city center, a number of people still remained trapped beneath the rubble of destroyed buildings. Many more people had been injured by falling debris. To deal with the disaster, hospitals throughout South Island were cleared to take in the many victims.

Highway surfaces were ripped open by the force of the shock waves that spread across the ground. ▷

Cars parked on the city's streets were flattened as buildings collapsed and fell.

Robyn O'Brien's family home was badly damaged by the 2011 earthquake in Christchurch, New Zealand:

"Every time we go back to our home we think, is it liveable, is it not liveable? Today we're thinking it's not liveable. But you've got to stay positive."

CHAOS DESCENDS

In the hours and days that followed the earthquake, Christchurch was a scene of chaos as police and emergency services did their best to free people from rubble and locate the 300 people who had been reported missing.

In the days following the earthquake, people worked round the clock to restore power and repair buildings.

Aftershocks Continue

As is the case with most severe earthquakes, aftershocks continued to hit the city for days after the main quake. Shocked and terrified people were told to leave the city until officials could assure them that the danger had passed.

The Earthquake and the Aftermath

FEB 22, 2011
12:51 p.m.
A large earthquake measuring 6.3 on the Richter scale strikes New Zealand, just 6 miles (10 km) from Christchurch.

1:20 p.m.
A National Crisis Center is set up to coordinate events.

2:07 p.m.
Police confirm "multiple fatalities."

2:32 p.m.
Police confirm that two buses have been crushed by falling masonry.

4:21 p.m.
Christchurch Mayor Bob Parker declares a state of emergency and asks for help.

6:20 p.m.
New Zealand Prime Minister John Key tells the media that "at least 65 people" are known to have died.

11:05 p.m.
Queen Elizabeth II says she is "utterly shocked" by the devastation and sends her thoughts to the people of Christchurch.

FEB 23, 2011
11:15 a.m.
300 people are still listed as missing.

11:27 a.m.
Fire services say that they are confident that 15 people are still alive, trapped inside an "air pocket" within the rubble of a collapsed television station office building.

A scene of devastation was left in the wake of the earthquake. A total of 185 people died in the event, making it New Zealand's worst-ever natural disaster.

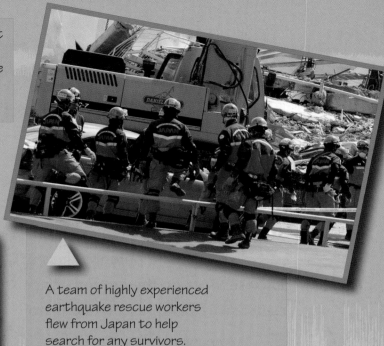

Author David Haywood was at home in Christchurch when the earthquake struck the city:

"The first jolt knocked me off my feet. A desktop computer landed near my head and exploded into parts. Every piece of furniture was moving. Time seemed to slow down. After the shaking stopped, there was a moment of silence, then a wailing of ambulance sirens."

A team of highly experienced earthquake rescue workers flew from Japan to help search for any survivors.

Years of Turmoil

New Zealand is still counting the cost of its worst natural disaster in decades. In total, 185 people died as a result of the earthquake, with 2,000 more injured. A series of heavy aftershocks continued to rock the city throughout 2011. It will be years before the country fully recovers.

11:30 a.m.
Prime Minister John Key declares a national state of emergency.

2:34 p.m.
A 54-year-old woman is pulled alive from the wreckage of a collapsed office block more than 24 hours after the earthquake. Some 90 minutes later, the last survivor is found in the rubble.

FEB 25, 2011
The death toll rises to 101. Police say over 200 people are still missing, presumed dead. The search and rescue team announce that they have rescued more than 70 people.

FEB 26, 2011
The official death toll rises. Some 55,000 homes are now without water.

MARCH 1, 2011
New Zealand stops for a 2 minute silence at 12:51 p.m., the moment a week earlier when the earthquake struck.

MARCH 2, 2011
The number of confirmed dead has risen to 160, with four bodies being recovered overnight. The New Zealand

national cricket team captain Daniel Vettori puts his entire collection of personal memorabilia up for auction to raise money to help the victims of the earthquake.

SEARCH AND RESCUE

In the minutes, hours, and days following an earthquake, it is vital to get emergency services to the affected area as quickly as possible to begin the search for survivors. In the United States, the response to an earthquake or other national disaster is coordinated by the Federal Emergency Management Agency. This organization quickly assesses the scale of the damage and potential loss of life, and coordinates emergency services on the ground. If needed, it also calls in specialist search and rescue teams from around the world.

Getting People Out Alive

Search and rescue specialists are used to dealing with the aftermath of major disasters. They are usually called on when buildings or other structures collapse. Their job is to find people among the rubble and make sure they get out alive. The work carries all kinds of potential dangers and requires specialist training.

Minutes can make the difference between life and death in the search for earthquake survivors. Rescue workers must operate quickly to ensure they find victims as quickly as possible.

Rescue Dogs

Specialists use various equipment and methods during a rescue operation. Sometimes they use specially trained dogs, called "sniffer dogs," to find people. The dogs are able to squeeze into small spaces in collapsed buildings that the rescuers cannot reach. If a sniffer dogs finds someone, the rescuers must quickly work out how to get them out alive. This can be a long and difficult process, but time is not on their side as the person may lack the air or water they need to stay alive. The rescuers must clear away enough debris to get to the casualty, without causing the rest of the building to collapse.

WORLD'S WORST

One of the biggest search and rescue operations the world has ever seen was launched following an earthquake in the Indian Ocean, close to the island of Sumatra, on December 26, 2004. The quake triggered a series of deadly tsunamis that killed 240,000 people in 14 countries.

BUILDING FOR THE FUTURE

Engineers and architects have spent a lot of time and money in recent years trying to make buildings earthquake proof. In the United States and Japan, both of which are prone to earthquakes, strict building regulations ensure that homes and offices are made as earthquake proof as possible. Existing buildings can be made more resistant to the effects of earthquakes, too. In a process called seismic retrofitting, features are added to the outside of buildings to help them stand up to the powerful ground shaking that occurs when earthquakes strike.

Adding Steel

In Japan and the United States, many older buildings, especially those made of concrete, have had new steel elements fitted to the outside of the structures. Steel is flexible and does not shatter like concrete, so it can withstand a certain amount of bending when the ground shakes.

The skyline of Tokyo, Japan, is dominated by enormous skyscrapers. The city features some of the world's most resilient and effective earthquake-proof architecture.

Pendulum Balls

Tall buildings such as skyscrapers are particularly at risk from earthquakes. To help them withstand the earth tremors, new skyscrapers are often fitted with a "mass dampener." This is a large steel ball that sits inside the tower. It is connected to the top and bottom of the inside of the tower by thick steel cables. In the event of an earthquake, the pendulum-like ball will stabilize the tower by reacting against the swaying that occurs when the ground shakes. In cities with a lot of skyscrapers, such as Hong Kong, Taipei, and Tokyo, this design feature has saved many lives.

Modern architecture is constantly evolving to improve the design of earthquake-proof buildings, such as this skyscraper in San Francisco.

WORLD'S WORST

One of the costliest earthquakes of all time took place in Hanshin, Japan, in 1995. More than 300,000 people were left homeless after the earthquake destroyed tens of thousands of buildings. The Japanese government says that Hanshin cost more than $100 billion to rebuild.

WHEN AN EARTHQUAKE STRIKES

Earthquakes can happen at any time. The constant slow and steady movement of the Earth's tectonic plates means that we will never be rid of these catastrophic events. Although scientists cannot prevent earthquakes from occuring, they are developing more and more effective technology to help predict them. With enough warning, populations in earthquake-prone areas can be evacuated before a major disaster occurs, which significantly reduces loss of life. Aid and rescue workers are also now better prepared than ever to know what to do in the event of a major earthquake.

Aid agencies, such as Unicef, train their workers to be ready to act quickly in the event of an earthquake in danger zones such as Indonesia.

Take Cover

The three places in the world thought to be most at risk of a major earthquake in the coming years are Indonesia, Chile, and California. Both Chile and California lie on the San Andreas Fault, where the Pacific and North American tectonic plates meet. The fault runs the entire length of North and South America, and anywhere along the fault could be at risk of suffering a catastrophic earthquake.

With much improved building techniques, it may be possible to avoid dramatic devastation such as that done to this building in the future.

A deadly earthquake took place in Messina, Italy, in 1908. More than 9 percent of buildings in the area were destroyed, and more than 140,000 people died. It is Europe's most destructive quake to date.

Be Prepared

There are some key steps to take in the event of an earthquake. People outdoors need to get away from power lines, trees, and buildings. These are the things most likely to fall or be damaged by an earthquake. Anyone indoors should stay away from windows, mirrors, and cupboards. If they have a sturdy table or desk, they should get underneath it. Another good place to take shelter is under doorways, which are one of the most solid parts of a house. No one can prevent earthquakes, but knowing how to react if one occurs can mean the difference between life and death.

GLOSSARY

aftershock: an earthquake that strikes after the main one and is smaller

body wave: a type of seismic wave that can only be detected underground

catastrophic: disastrous

debris: the remains of anything destroyed

epicenter: the central point of an earthquake where the strongest seismic effects are felt

fault line: the point at which two or more of Earth's tectonic plates meet

friction: the energy created when two objects rub together

geothermal electricity: electricity made using geothermal energy

geothermal energy: the earth's natural heat, which escapes from the core and occasionally makes its way to Earth's surface in the form of steam

induced seismicity: earthquake-like movements of the earth caused by human activity

magnitude: the size or extent of a thing; the strength of an earthquake

Richter scale: a system for measuring the magnitude of earthquakes

seismic activity: the movement or vibration of the earth's crust

seismic retrofitting: the process of strengthening buildings to make them able to withstand earthquakes

seismic waves: waves of energy that are released by an earthquake

seismograph: a machine used to detect seismic waves and record seismic activity

seismologist: a scientist who specializes in studying earthquakes

seismology: the science of studying earthquakes and other movements of the earth

shock waves: the waves of energy that flow outward from an earthquake's epicenter and make the ground shake

skyscraper: a very tall building, also called a "high rise" building

sniffer dogs: dogs that have been trained to detect people, drugs, or other items using their sense of smell

soil liquefaction: the process of previously solid ground turning to liquid following an earthquake

surface wave: a type of seismic wave that can be detected at the surface

tectonic plates: the huge plates of rock that cover the surface of the earth

tremor: slight shaking

FOR MORE INFORMATION

Books

Adamson, Heather. *Surviving an Earthquake*. Mankato, MN: Amicus Readers, 2012.

Gates, Alexander E. and David Ritchie. *The Encyclopedia of Earthquakes and Volcanoes*. New York, NY: Facts on File, 2007.

Griffey, Harriet. *Earthquakes and Other Natural Disasters*. New York, NY: DK Children, 2010.

Websites

Find out amazing facts about earthquakes, take a look at sensational earthquake photographs, and try out some fun activities too.
earthquake.usgs.gov/learn/kids

Find out more about earthquakes and where and why they occur.
thekidswindow.co.uk/news/earthquakes.htm

Read all about earthquakes, tectonic plates, fault lines, and tsunamis.
weatherwizkids.com/weather-earthquake.htm

INDEX